STRAIGHT ON TILL MORNING

Poems of the Imaginary World

STRAIGHT ON TILL MORNING

Poems of the Imaginary World

SELECTED BY *Helen Hill,*
Agnes Perkins, and Alethea Helbig

ILLUSTRATED BY *Ted Lewin*

Thomas Y. Crowell Company | New York

Library of Congress Cataloging in Publication Data
Main entry under title: Straight on till morning.
Includes index.
SUMMARY: A collection of nearly one hundred poems by modern
English and American poets.   1. Children's poetry,
English.   2. Children's poetry, American. [1. English
poetry—Collections. 2. American poetry—Collections]
I. Hill, Helen. II. Perkins, Agnes.
III. Helbig, Alethea. IV. Lewin, Ted, illus.
PN6110.C4S78   821'.008   76-55414
ISBN 0-690-01303-5
10 9 8 7 6 5 4 3 2 1

Contents

For these special children
Andrea, Nat, Thea, and Zephyr,
Heather and Howard
and all others who will venture
on the route to the Neverland:
"second to the right,
and straight on till morning."

Foreword

This collection of nearly one hundred poems is one of three in which we have gathered some of the best modern poems we could find for children. In this volume are poems about only one of the worlds the child lives in—the world of the imagination. We have saved for another volume the poems about his daily world, and for a third, the poems of contemplation and of word play which belong to his intellectual world. It is our hope that all these poems will give pleasure not only to the children themselves but also to the adults who read the poems to them. Many children, of course, can read the poems for themselves, but for the youngest, poetry is still a shared experience. That experience is happiest when both listener and reader can enjoy the same poems.

Two things have been important in our choice of poems: content and style. We have tried to choose poems whose content is within the range of a child's understanding, mindful that a child of twelve will understand more than a child of five. In a book of this sort there should be room to grow. If a few of these poems seem at first reading to be beyond the scope of some children, it is because of the mystery and potency of the language which gives us something to wonder about, something to return to and muse on. Does one have to be able to explicate in order to shiver under the spell of the last lines of Roethke's "The Small"?

> *What moves in grass I love—*
> *The dead will not lie still,*
> *And things throw light on things,*
> *And all the stones have wings.*

The styles of these poems are as various as the people who wrote them. Some are rhymed and strictly metered; some are not. All, however, are contemporary in their language and their tone, so that a child who picks up this book should not feel that poetry is a thing apart. Here, in the idiom of his own time, are poems that tell stories or describe strange people; poems that surprise us; poems full of mystery—like the ghostly voices whispering in the telephone:

> *You think they are from other wires.*
> *You think they are.*

Some poems are funny; some are serious; some are a little of both, like "The Bear Who Came to Dinner,"

> *dripping cold bees*
> *on a Queen Anne chair,*
> *moss to his ears*
> *and mildew for hair.*

And some will bring the comforting discovery that another person knows just how one feels and has been able to put that feeling into just the right words. Though we don't always recognize it, poetry is as basic to life as language itself. We don't all have the gift of the right language at the right time. We don't all have the gift of song; but we all like to join in the music. We all need to express ourselves and are best satisfied when we do it well. When we can't, we are fortunate to find poems which help us do it, whose language we would choose ourselves if we could.

Helen Hill
Agnes Perkins
Alethea Helbig

IN OUR
OWN WORLD

I'm Nobody!

I'm Nobody! Who are you?
Are you—Nobody—too?
Then there's a pair of us?
Don't tell! they'd advertise—you know!

How dreary—to be—Somebody!
How public—like a Frog—
To tell one's name—the livelong June—
To an admiring Bog!

Emily Dickinson

Halfway Down

Halfway down the stairs
Is a stair
Where I sit.
There isn't any
Other stair
Quite like
It.
I'm not at the bottom,
I'm not at the top;
So this is the stair
Where
I always
Stop.

Halfway up the stairs
Isn't up,
And isn't down.
It isn't in the nursery,
It isn't in the town.
And all sorts of funny thoughts
Run round my head:
"It isn't really
Anywhere!
It's somewhere else
Instead!"

A. A. Milne

Knoxville, Tennessee

I always like summer
best
you can eat fresh corn
from daddy's garden
and okra
and greens
and cabbage
and lots of
barbecue
and buttermilk
and homemade ice-cream
at the church picnic
and listen to
gospel music
outside
at the church
homecoming
and go to the mountains with
your grandmother
and go barefooted
and be warm
all the time
not only when you go to bed
and sleep
17 may 68

Nikki Giovanni

Song

I'd much rather sit there in the sun
watching the snow drip from the trees
and the milkman's footsteps fill up with water
and the shadow of the spruce tree branches waving
over the sparkle on the leftover snow
and the water dripping in front of my eyes
and the water dripping from the roof
from the bushes of sparkle the water is dripping
the water is dripping from my eyes it is not dripping
I'd much rather sit in the sun the sun
I'd much rather sit in the sun
listening to the shovels scraping
and the birds that whistle on the wires that are dripping
and the backporch is shining
the steam is floating up
the steam floats up around me like my breathing was before
and the maple tree is gleaming in the branches that are bare
above the backporch that is steaming
and I take off my shoes
I take off my stockings and
I sit in the sun I am sitting in the sun
I'd much rather sit here in the sun

Ruth Krauss

#4

Where my grandmother lived
there was always sweet potato pie
and thirds on green beans and
songs and words of how we'd
survived it all.
Blackness.
And the wind
a soft lull
in the pecan tree
whispered
Ethiopia
     Ethiopia, Ethiopia
E-th-io-piaaaaa!

Doughtry Long

A Visit to the Asylum

Once from a big, big building,
When I was small, small,
The queer folk in the windows
Would smile at me and call.

And in the hard wee gardens
Such pleasant men would hoe:
"Sir, may we touch the little girl's hair!"—
It was so red, you know.

They cut me coloured asters
With shears so sharp and neat,
They brought me grapes and plums and pears
And pretty cakes to eat.

And out of all the windows,
No matter where we went,
The merriest eyes would follow me
And make me compliment.

There were a thousand windows,
All latticed up and down.
And up to all the windows,
When we went back to town,

The queer folk put their faces,
As gentle as could be;
"Come again, little girl!" they called, and I
Called back, "You come see me!"

Edna St. Vincent Millay

The Turn of the Road

I was playing with my hoop along the road
Just where the bushes are, when, suddenly,
I heard a shout.—I ran away and stowed
Myself beneath a bush, and watched to see
What made the noise, and then, around the bend,
A woman came.

She was old!
She was wrinkle-faced! She had big teeth!—The end
Of her red shawl caught on a bush and rolled
Right off her, and her hair fell down.—Her face
Was white, and awful, and her eyes looked sick,
And she was talking queer.

"O God of Grace!"
Said she, "where is the child?" and flew back quick
The way she came, and screamed, and shook her hands!
... Maybe she was a witch from foreign lands!

James Stephens

8

I Had to Be Secret

I hid the peppermint
Under my pillow
In Grandmother's house
At the top of the stairs.

She wouldn't have minded,
But so I did;
I had to be secret,
For who would have known

I was not as I seemed,
I was double of heart,
I was angel and devil
On different days,

And who could have seen
So deep into me
As to say any moment
Which was which?

Mark Van Doren

The Sad Child's Song

Heavy, Heavy, hangs in my head.
Not over, over, not superfine.
In here, in my head, hangs Heavy, Heavy,
And nobody knows.
Dead down he hangs,
Nor sweats, nor swings;
Pure weight, pure lump, is Heavy in here,
Here in my head where nobody sees.
Not over, over, not lucky and fine,
Not something for others, laughing, to say
Is mine if I want it, mine, is mine.
What shall the owner do to redeem it?
I can do nothing with Heavy in here,
Here in my head; and nobody helps.
Dead weight he hangs,
Pure lump, nor swings.
Heavy, Heavy, is all I have.
Heavy, oh Heavy, is mine to keep.

Mark Van Doren

A Peck of Gold

Dust always blowing about the town,
Except when sea fog laid it down,
And I was one of the children told
Some of the blowing dust was gold.

All the dust the wind blew high
Appeared like gold in the sunset sky,
But I was one of the children told
Some of the dust was really gold.

Such was life in the Golden Gate:
Gold dusted all we drank and ate,
And I was one of the children told,
"We all must eat our peck of gold."

Robert Frost

The Small

The small birds swirl around;
The high cicadas chirr;
A towhee pecks the ground;
I look at the first star:
My heart held to its joy,
This whole September day.

The moon goes to the full;
The moon goes slowly down;
The wood becomes a wall.
Far things draw closer in.
A wind moves through the grass,
Then all is as it was.

What rustles in the fern?
I feel my flesh divide.
Things lost in sleep return
As if out of my side,
On feet that make no sound
Over the sodden ground.

The small shapes drowse: I live
To woo the fearful small;
What moves in grass I love—
The dead will not lie still,
And things throw light on things,
And all the stones have wings.

Theodore Roethke

FETCH ME FAR
AND FAR AWAY

Invocation

Dolphin plunge, fountain play.
Fetch me far and far away.

Fetch me far my nursery toys,
Fetch me far my mother's hand,
Fetch me far the painted joys.

And when the painted cock shall crow
Fetch me far my waking day
That I may dance before I go.

Fetch me far the breeze in the heat,
Fetch me far the curl of the wave,
Fetch me far the face in the street.

And when the other faces throng
Fetch me far a place in the mind
Where only truthful things belong.

Fetch me far a moon in a tree,
Fetch me far a phrase of the wind,
Fetch me far the verb To Be.

And when the last horn burns the hills
Fetch me far one draught of grace
To quench my thirst before it kills.

Dolphin plunge, fountain play.
Fetch me far and far away.

Louis MacNeice

The Paint Box

"Cobalt and umber and ultramarine,
Ivory black and emerald green—
What shall I paint to give pleasure to you?"
"Paint for me somebody utterly new."

"I have painted you tigers in crimson and white."
"The colours were good and you painted aright."
"I have painted the cook and a camel in blue
And a panther in purple." "You painted them true."

"Now mix me a colour that nobody knows,
And paint me a country where nobody goes.
And put in it people a little like you,
Watching a unicorn drinking the dew."

E. V. Rieu

Henry and Mary

Henry was a young king,
    Mary was his queen;
He gave her a snowdrop
    On a stalk of green.

Then all for his kindness
    And all for his care
She gave him a new-laid egg
    In the garden there.

"Love, can you sing?"
                "I cannot sing."
  "Or tell a tale?"
                "Not one I know."
"Then let us play at queen and king
    As down the garden walks we go."

                        Robert Graves

Unicorn

The Unicorn with the long white horn
    Is beautiful and wild.
He gallops across the forest green
So quickly that he's seldom seen
Where Peacocks their blue feathers preen
    And strawberries grow wild.
He flees the hunter and the hounds,
Upon black earth his white hoof pounds,
Over cold mountain streams he bounds
    And comes to a meadow mild;
There, when he kneels to take his nap,
He lays his head in a lady's lap
    As gently as a child.

William Jay Smith

A Sick Child

The postman comes when I am still in bed.
"Postman, what do you have for me today?"
I say to him. (But really I'm in bed.)
Then he says—what shall I have him say?

"This letter says that you are president
Of—this word here; it's a republic."
Tell them I can't answer right away.
"It's your duty." No, I'd rather just be sick.

Then he tells me there are letters saying everything
That I can think of that I want for them to say.
I say, "Well, thank you very much. Good-bye."
He is ashamed, and turns and walks away.

If I can think of it, it isn't what I want.
I want . . . I want a ship from some near star
To land in the yard, and beings to come out
And think to me: "So this is where you are!

Come." Except that they won't do,
I thought of them. . . . And yet somewhere there must be
Something that's different from everything.
All that I've never thought of—think of me!

Randall Jarrell

The Settlers

I was the father.
I crouched in deep grass
Behind the back kitchen
Turning the grindstone.
That was my job.

My sister was the mother,
Pounding grass for soup.
My cousins were the children.
They had to keep building,
Trampling the grass
To make more rounded green rooms.

No one could see me
But I worked until sundown
Because only the grass I had ground
Was real food, real medicine,
Real fuel to keep us warm.
In autumn we used maple leaves,
In winter, snow.

Judith Hemschemeyer

Merry-Go-Round

Horses in front of me,
Horses behind,
But mine is the best one,
He never looks down.
He rises and falls
As if there were waves,
But he never goes under,
Oh, music, oh, mine.

He is steady and strong,
And he knows I am here,
He says he is glad
That I picked him to ride.
But he hasn't a name.
I told him my own,
And he only went faster,
Oh, music, oh, mine.

Around and around,
And the people out there
Don't notice how happy
I am, I am.
The others are too,
But I am the most,
The most, the most,
Oh, music, oh, mine.

Mark Van Doren

The Centaur

The summer that I was ten—
Can it be there was only one
summer that I was ten? It must

have been a long one then—
each day I'd go out to choose
a fresh horse from my stable

which was a willow grove
down by the old canal.
I'd go on my two bare feet.

But when, with my brother's jack-knife,
I had cut me a long limber horse
with a good thick knob for a head,

and peeled him slick and clean
except a few leaves for the tail,
and cinched my brother's belt

around his head for a rein,
I'd straddle and canter him fast
up the grass bank to the path,

trot along in the lovely dust
that talcumed over his hoofs,
hiding my toes, and turning

his feet to swift half-moons.
The willow knob with the strap
jouncing between my thighs

was the pommel and yet the poll
of my nickering pony's head.
My head and my neck were mine,

yet they were shaped like a horse.
My hair flopped to the side
like the mane of a horse in the wind.

My forelock swung in my eyes,
my neck arched and I snorted.
I shied and skittered and reared,

stopped and raised my knees,
pawed at the ground and quivered.
My teeth bared as we wheeled

and swished through the dust again.
I was the horse and the rider,
and the leather I slapped to his rump

spanked my own behind.
Doubled, my two hoofs beat
a gallop along the bank,

the wind twanged in my mane,
my mouth squared to the bit.
And yet I sat on my steed

quiet, negligent riding,
my toes standing the stirrups,
my thighs hugging his ribs.

At a walk we drew up to the porch.
I tethered him to a paling.
Dismounting, I smoothed my skirt

and entered the dusky hall.
My feet on the clean linoleum
left ghostly toes in the hall.

Where have you been? said my mother.
Been riding, I said from the sink,
and filled me a glass of water.

What's that in your pocket? she said.
Just my knife. It weighted my pocket
and stretched my dress awry.

Go tie back your hair, said my mother,
and *Why is your mouth all green?*
*Rob Roy, he pulled some clover
as we crossed the field,* I told her.

May Swenson

The Bedpost

Sleepy Betsy from her pillow
  Sees the post and ball
Of her sister's wooden bedstead
  Shadowed on the wall.

Now this grave young warrior standing
  With uncovered head
Tells her stories of old battle
  As she lies in bed:

How the Emperor and the Farmer,
  Fighting knee to knee,
Broke their swords but whirled their scabbards
  Till they gained the sea.

How the ruler of that shore
  Foully broke his oath,
Gave them beds in his sea cave,
  Then stabbed them both.

How the daughters of the Emperor,
  Diving boldly through,
Caught and killed their father's murderer
  Old Cro-bar-cru.

How the Farmer's sturdy sons
  Fought the Giant Gog,
Threw him into Stony Cataract
  In the land of Og.

Will and Abel were their names,
    Though they went by others:
He could tell ten thousand stories
    Of these lusty brothers.

How the Emperor's elder daughter
    Fell in love with Will
And went with him to the Court of Venus
    Over Hoo Hill;

How Gog's wife encountered Abel
    Whom she hated most,
Stole away his arms and helmet,
    Turned him to a post.

As a post he shall stay rooted
    For yet many years,
Until a maiden shall release him
    With pitying tears.

But Betsy likes the bloodier stories,
    Clang and clash of fight,
And Abel wanes with the spent candle—
    "Sweetheart, good-night!"

Robert Graves

Rebels from Fairy Tales

We are the frogs who will not turn to princes.
We will not change our green and slippery skin
for one so lily-pale and plain, so smooth
it seems to have no grain. We will not leave
our leap, our spring, accordion. We have
seen ourselves in puddles, and we like
our grin. Men are so up and down, so thin
they look like walking trees. Their knees seem stiff,
and we have seen men shooting hares and deer.
They're queer . . . they even war with one another!
They've stretched too far from earth and natural things
for us to admire. We prefer to lie
close to the water looking at the sky
reflected; contemplating how the sun,
Great Rana, can thrust his yellow, webbed foot
through all the elements in a giant jump;
can poke the bottom of the brook; warm
the stumps for us to sit upon; and heat
our backs. Men have forgotten to relax.
They bring their noisy boxes, and the blare
insults the air. We cannot hear the cheer
of crickets, nor our own dear booming chugs.
Frogs wouldn't ever eat men's legs.
We scorn their warm, dry princesses. We're proud
of our own bug-eyed brides with bouncing strides.
Keep your magic. We are not such fools.
Here is the ball without a claim on it.
We may begin from the same tadpoles, but
we've thought a bit, and will not turn to men.

Hyacinthe Hill

The Cloud-Mobile

Above my face is a map
where continents form and fade.
Blue countries, made
on a white sea, are erased;
white countries are traced
on a blue sea.

It is a map that moves
faster than real
but so slow;
only my watching proves
that island has being,
or that bay.

It is a model of time;
mountains are wearing away,
coasts cracking, the ocean
spills over, then new
hills heap into view
with river-cuts of blue between them.

It is a map of change:
this is the way things are
with a stone or a star.
This is the way things go,
hard or soft,
swift or slow.

May Swenson

Warning to Children

Children, if you dare to think
Of the greatness, rareness, muchness,
Fewness of this precious only
Endless world in which you say
You live, you think of things like this:
Blocks of slate enclosing dappled
Red and green, enclosing tawny
Yellow nets, enclosing white
And black acres of dominoes,
Where a neat brown paper parcel
Tempts you to untie the string.
In the parcel a small island,
On the island a large tree,
On the tree a husky fruit.
Strip the husk and pare the rind off:
In the kernel you will see
Blocks of slate enclosed by dappled
Red and green, enclosed by tawny
Yellow nets, enclosed by white
And black acres of dominoes,
Where the same brown paper parcel—
Children, leave the string alone!
For who dares undo the parcel
Finds himself at once inside it,
On the island, in the fruit,
Blocks of slate about his head,
Finds himself enclosed by dappled

Green and red, enclosed by yellow
Tawny nets, enclosed by black
And white acres of dominoes,
With the same brown paper parcel
Still untied upon his knee.
And, if he then should dare to think
Of the fewness, muchness, rareness,
Greatness of this endless only
Precious world in which he says
He lives—he then unties the string.

Robert Graves

FUNNY AND FABULOUS FRIENDS

Mr. Tom Narrow

A scandalous man
   Was Mr. Tom Narrow,
He pushed his grandmother
   Round in a barrow.
And he called out loud
   As he rang his bell,
"Grannies to sell!
   Old grannies to sell!"

The neighbours said,
   As they passed them by,
"This poor old lady
   We will not buy.
He surely must be
   A mischievous man
To try for to sell
   His own dear Gran."

"Besides," said another,
   "If you ask me,
She'd be very small use
   That I can see."
"You're right," said a third,
   "And no mistake—
A very poor bargain
   She'd surely make."

So Mr. Tom Narrow
   He scratched his head,
And he sent his grandmother
   Back to bed;
And he rang his bell
   Through all the town
Till he sold his barrow
   For half a crown.

James Reeves

The Man in the Onion Bed

I met a man in an onion bed.
He was crying so hard his eyes were red.
And the tears ran off the end of his nose
As he ate his way down the onion rows.

He ate and he cried, but for all his tears
He sang: "Sweet onions, oh my dears!
I love you, I do, and you love me,
But you make me as sad as a man can be."

"Why are you crying," I asked. And he
Stopped his singing and looked at me.
"I love my onions, I do," he said,
"And I hate to pull them out of bed.
And wouldn't it make *you* want to weep
To eat them up while they're still asleep?"

"Then why don't you wake them?"
                                    "Ah," he said,
"Onions are best when they're still in bed!"
And he cried and he ate and he ate and he cried
Till row by row and side to side
He ate till there were no more, then sat
And started to cry again for that.

He cried till his coat and shoes were wet.
For all I know, he is crying yet.

John Ciardi

36

Lighthearted William

Lighthearted William twirled
his November moustaches
and, half dressed, looked
from the bedroom window
upon the spring weather.

Heigh-ya! sighed he gaily
leaning out to see
up and down the street
where a heavy sunlight
lay beyond some blue shadows.

Into the room he drew
his head again and laughed
to himself quietly
twirling his green moustaches.

William Carlos Williams

A Lady Comes to an Inn

Three strange men came to the inn.
One was a black man, pocked and thin,
one was brown with a silver knife,
and one brought with him a beautiful wife.

That lovely woman had hair as pale
as French champagne or finest ale,
that lovely woman was long and slim
as a young white birch or a maple limb.

Her face was like cream, her mouth was a rose,
what language she spoke nobody knows,
but sometimes she'd scream like a cockatoo
and swear wonderful oaths that nobody knew.

Her great silk skirts like a silver bell
down to her little bronze slippers fell,
and her low-cut gown showed a dove on its nest
in blue tattooing across her breast.

Nobody learned the lady's name,
nor the marvelous land from which she came,
but still they tell through the countryside
the tale of those men and that beautiful bride.

Elizabeth Coatsworth

My Sister Jane

And I say nothing—no, not a word
About our Jane. Haven't you heard?
She's a bird, a bird, a bird, a bird.
Oh it never would do to let folks know
My sister's nothing but a great big crow.

Each day (we daren't send her to school)
She pulls on stockings of thick blue wool
To make her pin crow legs look right,
Then fits a wig of curls on tight,
And dark spectacles—a huge pair
To cover her very crowy stare.
Oh it never would do to let folks know
My sister's nothing but a great big crow.

When visitors come she sits upright
(With her wings and her tail tucked out of sight).
They think her queer but extremely polite.
Then when the visitors have gone
She whips out her wings and with her wig on
Whirls through the house at the height of your head—
Duck, duck, or she'll knock you dead.
Oh it never would do to let folks know
My sister's nothing but a great big crow.

At meals whatever she sees she'll stab it—
Because she's a crow and that's a crow habit.
My mother says, "Jane! Your manners! Please!"
Then she'll sit quietly on the cheese,
Or play the piano nicely by dancing on the keys—
Oh it never would do to let folks know
My sister's nothing but a great big crow.

Ted Hughes

Tony the Turtle

Tony was a Turtle
   Very much at ease,
Swimming in the sunshine
   Through the summer seas,
And feeding on the fishes
Irrespective of their wishes,
With a "By your leave" and "Thank you"
   And a gentlemanly squeeze.

Tony was a Turtle
   Who loved a civil phrase;
Anxious and obliging,
   Sensitive to praise.
And to hint that he was snappy
Made him thoroughly unhappy;
For Tony was a Turtle
   With most engaging ways.

Tony was a Turtle
   Who thought, before he fed,
Of other people's comfort,
   And as he ate them said:
"If I seem a little grumpy,
It is *not* that you are lumpy."
   For Tony was a Turtle
   Delicately bred.

E. V. Rieu

A Trueblue Gentleman

This gentleman the charming duck
Quack quack says he
My tail's on
Fire, but he's only kidding

You can tell that
By his grin
He's one big grin, from wobbly
Feet to wobbly tail
Quack quack he tells us

Tail's on fire again

Ah yes
This charming gentleman the duck
With
His quaint alarms and
Trick of walking like a
Drunken hat
Quack quack says he

There's your fried egg

Kenneth Patchen

The Haughty Snail-King

(What Uncle William Told the Children)

Twelve snails went walking after night.
They'd creep an inch or so,
Then stop and bug their eyes
And blow.
Some folks . . . are . . . deadly . . . slow.
Twelve snails went walking yestereve,
Led by their fat old king.
They were so dull their princeling had
No sceptre, robe or ring—
Only a paper cap to wear
When nightly journeying.

This king-snail said: "I feel a thought
Within . . . It blossoms soon. . . .
O little courtiers of mine, . . .
I crave a pretty boon . . . ,
Oh, yes . . . (High thoughts with effort come
And well-bred snails are ALMOST dumb.)
"I wish I had a yellow crown
As glistering . . . as . . . the moon."

Vachel Lindsay

The Lady and the Bear

A Lady came to a Bear by a Stream.
"O why are you fishing that way?
Tell me, dear Bear there by the Stream,
Why are you fishing that way?"

"I am what is known as a Biddly Bear,—
That's why I'm fishing this way.
We Biddly's are Pee-culiar Bears.
And so,—I'm fishing this way.

"And besides, it seems there's a Law:
A most, most exactious Law
Says a Bear
Doesn't dare
Doesn't dare
Doesn't DARE
Use a Hook or a Line,
Or an old piece of Twine,
Not even the end of his Claw, Claw, Claw,
Not even the end of his Claw.
Yes, a Bear has to fish with his Paw, Paw, Paw.
A Bear has to fish with his Paw."

"O it's Wonderful how with a flick of your Wrist,
You can fish out a fish, out a fish, out a fish,
If *I* were a fish I just couldn't resist
You, when you are fishing that way, that way,
When you are fishing that way."

And at that the Lady slipped from the Bank
And fell in the Stream still clutching a Plank,
But the Bear just sat there until she Sank;
As he went on fishing his way, his way,
As he went on fishing his way.

Theodore Roethke

Self-portrait, As a Bear

Here is a fat animal, a bear
that is partly a dodo.
Ridiculous wings hang at his shoulders
while he plods in the brickyards
at the edge of the city, smiling
and eating flowers. He eats them
because he loves them
because they are beautiful
because they love him.
It is eating flowers which makes him fat.
He carries his huge stomach
over the gutters of damp leaves
in the parking lots in October,
but inside that paunch
he knows there are fields of lupine
and meadows of mustard and poppy.
He encloses sunshine.
Winds bend the flowers
in combers across the valley,
birds hang on the stiff wind,
at night there are showers, and the sun
lifts through a haze every morning
of the summer in the stomach.

Donald Hall

Alligator on the Escalator

Through the revolving door
Of a department store
There slithered an alligator.

When he came to the escalator,
He stepped upon the track with great dexterity;
His tail draped over the railing,
And he clicked his teeth in glee:
    "Yo, I'm off on the escalator,
    Excited as I can be!
    It's a *moving* experience,
    As you can plainly see.
    On the moving stair I go anywhere,
    I rise to the top
    Past outerwear, innerwear,
    Dinnerwear, thinnerwear—
    Then down to the basement with bargains galore,
    Then back on the track to the top once more!
    Oh, I may ride the escalator
    Until closing time or later,
    So tell the telephone operator
    To call Mrs. Albert Q. Alligator
    And tell her to take a hot mud bath
    And not to wait up for me!"

Eve Merriam

OUT OF
THIS WORLD

The Two Witches

O sixteen hundred and ninety one,
Never was year so well begun,
Backsy-forsy and inside out,
The best of all years to ballad about.

On the first fine day of January
I ran to my sweetheart Margery
And tossed her over the roof so far
That down she fell like a shooting star.

But when we two had frolicked and kissed
She clapped her fingers about my wrist
And tossed me over the chimney stack,
And danced on me till my bones did crack.

Then, when she had laboured to ease my pain,
We sat by the stile of Robin's Lane,
She in a hare and I in a toad
And puffed at the clouds till merry they glowed.

We spelled our loves until close of day.
I wished her good-night and walked away,
But she put out a tongue that was long and red
And swallowed me down like a crumb of bread.

Robert Graves

Old Ben Golliday

Old Ben Golliday
Jumped off the wagon box,
And trotted with his horses,
Clop, clop, clop.

Old Ben Golliday
Was angry with his little wife,
And didn't see her bonnet strings
Fly, fly, fly.

Didn't look around
At the thank-you-mam, thank-you-mam,
Didn't see her somersault
High, high, high.

Old Ben Golliday
Trotted to the barn door,
And went in with his horses
To sleep, sleep, sleep.

Old Ben Golliday,
Dozing in the manger there,
Don't you know your little wife
Sits in the sky?

Old Ben Golliday,
Who will get your dinner now,
Who will sew your buttons on?
My, my, my!

Mark Van Doren

Jim Jay

Do diddle di do,
  Poor Jim Jay
Got stuck fast
  In Yesterday.
Squinting he was,
  On cross-legs bent,
Never heeding
  The wind was spent.
Round veered the weathercock,
  The sun drew in—
And stuck was Jim
  Like a rusty pin. . . .
We pulled and we pulled
  From seven till twelve,
Jim, too frightened
  To help himself.
But all in vain.
  The clock struck one,
And there was Jim
  A little bit gone.
At half-past five
  You scarce could see
A glimpse of his flapping
  Handkerchee.
And when came noon,
  And we climbed sky-high,

Jim was a speck
    Slip—slipping by.
Come to-morrow,
    The neighbours say,
He'll be past crying for:
    Poor Jim Jay.

    Walter de la Mare

Riley

Down in the water meadows Riley
Spread his wash on the bramble-thorn,
Sat, one foot in the moving water,
Bare as the day that he was born.

Candid was his curling whisker,
Brown his body as an old tree limb,
Blue his eye as the jay above him
Watching him watch the minnows swim.

Four stout sticks for walls had Riley,
His roof was a rusty piece of tin,
As snug in the lee of a thorny hedgerow
He watched the seasons out and in.

He paid no rates, he paid no taxes,
His lamp was the moon hung in the tree.
Though many an ache and pain had Riley
He envied neither you nor me.

Many a friend from bush or burrow
To Riley's hand would run or fly,
And soft he'd sing and sweet he'd whistle
Whatever the weather in the sky.

Till one winter's morning Riley
From the meadow vanished clean.
Gone was the rusty tin, the timber,
As if old Riley had never been.

What strange secret had old Riley?
Where did he come from? Where did he go?
Why was his heart as light as summer?
"Never know now," said the jay. "Never know."

Charles Causley

Rebecca, Who slammed Doors for Fun and Perished Miserably

A Trick that everyone abhors
In Little Girls is slamming Doors.
A Wealthy Banker's Little Daughter
Who lived in Palace Green, Bayswater
(By name Rebecca Offendort),
Was given to this Furious Sport.

She would deliberately go
And Slam the door like Billy-Ho!
To make her Uncle Jacob start.
She was not really bad at heart,
But only rather rude and wild:
She was an aggravating child. . . .

It happened that a Marble Bust
Of Abraham was standing just
Above the Door this little Lamb

Had carefully prepared to Slam,
And Down it came! It knocked her flat!
It laid her out! She looked like that.

Her funeral Sermon (which was long
And followed by a Sacred Song)
Mentioned her Virtues, it is true,
But dwelt upon her Vices too,
And showed the Dreadful End of One
Who goes and slams the door for Fun.

The children who were brought to hear
The awful Tale from far and near
Were much impressed, and inly swore
They never more would slam the Door.
—As often they had done before.

Hilaire Belloc

The Cat Heard the Cat-Bird

One day, a fine day, a high-flying-sky day,
A cat-bird, a fat bird, a fine fat cat-bird
Was sitting and singing on a stump by the highway.
Just sitting. And singing. Just that. But a cat heard.

A thin cat, a grin-cat, a long thin grin-cat
Came creeping the sly way by the highway to the stump.
"O cat-bird, the cat heard! O cat-bird scat!
The grin-cat is creeping! He's going to jump!"

—One day, a fine day, a high-flying-sky day
A fat cat, yes, that cat we met as a thin cat
Was napping, cat-napping, on a stump by the highway,
And even in his sleep you could see he was a grin-cat.

Why was he grinning?   —He must have had a dream.
What made him fat?   —A pan full of cream.
What about the cat-bird?   —What bird, dear?
I don't see any cat-bird here.

John Ciardi

The Witch's Cat

"My magic is dead," said the witch. "I'm astounded
That people can fly to the moon and around it.
It used to be mine and the cat's till they found it.
My broomstick is draughty, I snivel with cold
As I ride to the stars. I'm painfully old,
    And so is my cat;
    But planet-and-space-ship,
    Rocket or race-ship
  Never shall part me from that."

She wrote an advertisement, "Witch in a fix
Willing to part with the whole bag of tricks,
Going cheap at the price at eighteen and six."
But no one was ready to empty his coffers
For out-of-date rubbish. There weren't any offers—
    Except for the cat.
    "But planet-and-space-ship,
    Rocket or race-ship
  Never shall part me from that."

The tears trickled fast, not a sentence she spoke
As she stamped on her broom and the brittle stick broke,
And she dumped in a dustbin her hat and her cloak,
Then clean disappeared, leaving no prints;
And no one at all has set eyes on her since
    Or her tired old cat.
    "But planet-and-space-ship,
    Rocket or race-ship
  Never shall part me from that."

Ian Serraillier

who knows if the moon's

who knows if the moon's
a balloon, coming out of a keen city
in the sky—filled with pretty people?
(and if you and i should

get into it, if they
should take me and take you into their balloon,
why then
we'd go up higher with all the pretty people

than houses and steeples and clouds:
go sailing
away and away sailing into a keen
city which nobody's ever visited, where

always
        it's
            Spring)and everyone's
in love and flowers pick themselves

E. E. Cummings

The Hatch

I found myself one day
cracking the shell of sky,
peering into a place
beyond mere universe.

I broke from egg of here
into anotherwhere
wider than worldly home
I was emerging from.

I breathed, I took a step,
I looked around, and up,
and saw another lining
inside a further sky.

Norma Farber

Flight

The doctor said, Count to ten.
One (a funny mask on my face),
two (I knew the doctor was kind but)
three, they promised ice—, four,
I can't, five, say five,

                           and I

was flying up over the roof
with crowds of red and blue balloons
like the time I sneaked up in the air
with my uncle in his scalawag plane
and looked below to the ribbon rivers
and fields of puzzles fitted together—

and I still have never told my mother
that I flew that day, that I flew away,
a plane
        a kite
                a balloon
                        a child
beyond her worried hands.

                       Ruth Whitman

Flight of the Roller-Coaster

Once more around should do it, the man confided . . .

And sure enough, when the roller-coaster reached the peak
Of the giant curve above me—screech of its wheels
Almost drowned by the shriller cries of the riders—

Instead of the dip and plunge with its landslide of screams
It rose in the air like a movieland magic carpet, some wonder-
    ful bird,

And without fuss or fanfare swooped slowly across the amuse-
    ment park,
Over Spook's Castle, ice-cream booths, shooting-gallery; and
    losing no height

Made the last yards above the beach, where the cucumber-cool
Brakeman in the last seat saluted
A lady about to change from her bathing-suit.

Then, as many witnesses duly reported, headed leisurely over
    the water,
Disappearing mysteriously all too soon behind a low-lying
    flight of clouds.

Raymond Souster

The Pinwheel's Song

Seven around the moon go up
   (Light the fuse and away we go)
Two in silver and two in red
And two in blue, and one went dead.
   Six around the moon.

Six around the moon go up,
   Six around the moon.
Whirl in silver, whirl in blue,
Sparkle in red, and one burned through.
   Five around the moon.

Five around the moon go up
   (Rocketing up to the moon)
Sparkle and shine in a wonderful flare,
Till one went dead a mile in the air.
   Four around the moon.

Four to rocket around the moon.
   (Look at the crowds below!)
Four gone zooming above the sea,
But one got lost, and that makes three.
   Three around the moon.

Three around the moon go up.
   (Don't bump into a star!)
Silver and Red and whistling loud,
But Blue crashed into a thundercloud.
   Two around the moon.

Two around the moon, well, well.
  Two to reach the moon.
But Silver turned left, and Red turned right,
And CRASH! they splattered all over the night
  Falling away from the moon.

None of them going as far as the moon?
  None of them going that far?
Quick! Somebody light me another fuse.
But I'm all burned out . . . it's just no use. . . .
    It's really
            too far
                to
                    the
                        moo. . . .

                                John Ciardi

MYSTERIES

Laly, Laly

There were two great trees
And a path between,
With a door at the end
That said "Come in,
My name is Laly.
Whoever you are,
Come gaily, gaily,
Without any fear."

"Who's Laly?" we said,
And didn't knock.
"Who's Laly?"—so loud,
Our voices came back.
Nobody knew
Who Laly was,
Or whether she listened
Inside the house.

Laly, Laly,
Whatever you said—
Forgive me truly—
We were afraid.
You shouldn't have told us
Not to be,
Laly, Laly,
So young were we.

Mark Van Doren

Green Candles

"There's someone at the door," said gold candlestick:
"Let her in quick, let her in quick!"
"There is a small hand groping at the handle.
Why don't you turn it?" asked green candle.

"Don't go, don't go," said the Hepplewhite chair,
"Lest you find a strange lady there."
"Yes, stay where you are," whispered the white wall:
"There is nobody there at all."

"I know her little foot," gray carpet said:
"Who but I should know her light tread?"
"She shall come in," answered the open door,
"And not," said the room, "go out any more."

Humbert Wolfe

Mistletoe

Sitting under the mistletoe
(Pale-green, fairy mistletoe),
One last candle burning low,
All the sleepy dancers gone,
Just one candle burning on,
Shadows lurking everywhere:
Some one came, and kissed me there.

Tired I was; my head would go
Nodding under the mistletoe
(Pale-green, fairy mistletoe);
No footsteps came, no voice, but only,
Just as I sat there, sleepy, lonely,
Stooped in the still and shadowy air
Lips unseen—and kissed me there.

Walter de la Mare

Where Did He Run To?

Where did he run to,
That old rooster?
Fox, fox,
How fast did he run?

Where is the mule gone,
That old rope-tail?
Manger, manger,
Where is the mule?

Where are the kittens
The old black cat had?
Blinker, Blinker,
Where are the kittens?

Where does the dog sleep,
That old shepherd?
Lambs on the mountain,
Where is your dog?

Where is the big boy
That swung on the gatepost?
Bedclothes, bedclothes,
Where is the boy?

Mark Van Doren

Ghost Boy

He came down the old road
Where nobody lives now—
The houses are but bramble holes,
The lilacs have been shaded out—
He skipped over fallen limbs,
He whistled to the bright birds,
He came down the dead road
And said his name, I swear he did,
Was Chipman, which it couldn't be,
For never in a hundred years
Have any Chipmans been up there.
Chipman? No. But on he trotted,
Barefoot, in tattered pants,
His eyes wide open, looking
Left and right for something low,
Something that he had to see;
And stopped where the school was.
Nothing but a place now,
Nothing, even stones, there.
Nevertheless he turned in,
Took off his cap, and sat down—
And disappeared in sudden mist.
It cleared, but he was clean gone;
And still is, although I hear
Some days a bell ring,
Sometimes a pencil tap.

Mark Van Doren

The Green Train

The Blue Train for the South—but the Green Train for us.
Nobody knows when the Green Train departs.
Nobody sees her off. There is no noise; no fuss;
No luggage on the Green Train;
No whistle when she starts.
But quietly at the right time they wave the green light
And she slides past the platform and plunges into the night.

Wonderful people walking down the long Green Train,
As the engine gathers speed.
And voices talking.
"Where does she go to, Guard?"
Where indeed?
But what does it matter
So long as the night is starred?
Who cares for time, and who cares for the place,
So long as the Green Train thunders on into space?

E. V. Rieu

Long Distance

Sometimes when you watch the fire
ashes glow and gray
the way the sun turned cold on spires
in winter in the town back home
so far away.

Sometimes on the telephone
the one you hear goes far
and ghostly voices whisper in.
You think they are from other wires.
You think they are.

William Stafford

Shadow-Bride

There was a man who dwelt alone,
    as day and night went past
he sat as still as carven stone,
    and yet no shadow cast.
The white owls perched upon his head
    beneath the winter moon;
they wiped their beaks and thought him dead
    under the stars of June.

There came a lady clad in grey
    in the twilight shining:
one moment she would stand and stay,
    her hair with flowers entwining.
He woke, as had he sprung of stone,
    and broke the spell that bound him;
he clasped her fast, both flesh and bone,
    and wrapped her shadow round him.

There never more she walks her ways
    by sun or moon or star;
she dwells below where neither days
    nor any nights there are.
But once a year when caverns yawn
    and hidden things awake,
they dance together then till dawn
    and a single shadow make.

J. R. R. Tolkien

The Horn

"Oh, hear you a horn, mother, behind the hill?
My body's blood runs bitter and chill.
The seven long years have passed, mother, passed,
And here comes my rider at last, at last.
I hear his horse now, and soon I must go.
How dark is the night, mother, cold the winds blow.
How fierce the hurricane over the deep sea!
For a seven years' promise he comes to take me."

"Stay at home, daughter, stay here and hide.
I will say you have gone, I will tell him you died.
I am lonely without you, your father is old;
Warm is our hearth, daughter, but the world is cold."

"Oh mother, Oh mother, you must not talk so.
In faith I promised, and for faith I must go,
For if that old promise I should not keep,
For seven long years, mother, I would not sleep.
Seven years my blood would run bitter and chill
To hear that sad horn, mother, behind the hill.
My body once frozen by such a shame
Would never be warmed, mother, at your hearth's flame.
But round my true heart shall the arms of the storm
For ever be folded, protecting and warm."

James Reeves

Middle Ages

I heard a clash, and a cry,
And a horseman fleeing the wood.
The moon hid in a cloud.
Deep in shadow I stood.
    "Ugly work!" thought I,
Holding my breath.
    "Men must be cruel and proud,
    Jousting for death."

With gusty glimmering shone
The moon; and the wind blew colder.
A man went over the hill,
Bent to his horse's shoulder.
    "Time for me to be gone" . . .
Darkly I fled.
    Owls in the wood were shrill,
    And the moon sank red.

                    Siegfried Sassoon

The Beast

I came to a great door,
Its lintel overhung
With burr, bramble, and thorn;
And when it swung, I saw
A meadow, lush and green.

And there a great beast played,
A sportive, aimless one,
A shred of bone its horn,
And colloped round with fern.
It looked at me; it stared.

Swaying, I took its gaze;
Faltered; rose up again;
Rose but to lurch and fall,
Hard, on the gritty sill,
I lay; I languished there.

When I raised myself once more,
The great round eyes had gone.
The long lush grass lay still;
And I wept there, alone.

Theodore Roethke

WHAT'S THERE IN THE DARK?

hist   whist

hist   whist
little ghostthings
tip-toe
twinkle-toe

little twitchy
witches and tingling
goblins
hob-a-nob   hob-a-nob

little hoppy happy
toad in tweeds
tweeds
little itchy mousies

with scuttling
eyes   rustle and run   and
hidehidehide
whisk

whisk   look out for the old woman
with the wart on her nose
what she'll do to yer
nobody knows

for she knows the devil   ooch
the devil   ouch
the devil
ach   the great

green
dancing
devil
devil

devil
devil

          wheeEEE

          E. E. Cummings

The Man from the Woods

The man from the woods
    Climbed out of my well
With some very strange goods
    He wanted to sell.

I was out on the farm
    And all alone
When I saw one arm
    Reach over the stone

Like a brambly shoot
    Or a prickly hedge.
And then one foot
    Grew over the edge,

Like roots when they grow
    Along the ground.
It frightened me so
    I turned around

And started to run,
    But he started to sing
In a voice like a pun
    With a quibbledy ring.

A two-tone voice
	Like a brook on a hill.
It was half just noise,
	And half bird-trill:

"Come buy, come buy what I have to sell.
	What's deepest, darkest, and longest gone
Out of the sun and down through the well
	To the little dark places in stone.

I have veins of iron and dusts of gold.
	Moss cake, root hair, beetle shell.
The last ball Rip Van Winkle bowled.
	And somewhere the first as well.

I have mildew glue and limestone twists.
	Darks of caves and water sound.
Bat-fur, fox-fire, mandrake fists.
	And all the lost buttons that no one has found.

I have rattlesnake rattles and dinosaur bone.
	Hearts of sulfur and mushroom seed.
Good fern jelly and honey stone.
	Come buy whatever you need."

He sang so small
      And so far and near,
And his voice was all
      So muffled and clear,

So twice-at-once,
      As I think I've said,
That I felt like a dunce
      For being afraid.

So I turned around
      To see his face.
—And there wasn't a sound!
      There wasn't a trace!

Whoever he was,
      He had been and gone.
But there on the grass
      Was a milk-white stone.

And as red a rose
      As ever grew.
Though I don't suppose
      You'll believe it's true.

                  John Ciardi

In the Orchard

There was a giant by the Orchard Wall
Peeping about on this side and on that,
And feeling in the trees. He was as tall
As the big apple tree, and twice as fat:
His beard poked out, all bristly-black and there
Were leaves and gorse and heather in his hair.

He held a blackthorn club in his right hand,
And plunged the other into every tree,
Searching for something—You could stand
Beside him and not reach up to his knee
So big he was—I trembled lest he should
Come trampling, round-eyed, down to where I stood.

I tried to get away.—But, as I slid
Under a bush, he saw me, and he bent
Down deep at me, and said, *"Where is she hid?"*
I pointed over there, and off he went—

But, while he searched, I turned and simply flew
Round by the lilac bushes back to you!

James Stephens

The Bear Who Came to Dinner

Where he rows the dark
any door will do.
You can't keep him out;
he'll cellar through
keyhole or crack
on his bearded knees
if yellow once twangs
in your black like bees.
You can't keep him out,
yet you can't have him in
like a cave in the house,
haunches and chin
dripping cold bees
on a Queen Anne chair,
moss to his ears
and mildew for hair.
He'll thumb back your lids
in sleep for a lark,
breed moths in your bed,
and snore like a harp.
There's nothing he won't,
and nothing he will,
but he'll lug the whole dark
across your door sill.

Adrien Stoutenburg

Nightmare of Mouse

It was there, but I said it couldn't be true in daylight.
It was there, but I said it was only a trick of starlight.
It was there, but I said to believe it would take a fool,
And I wasn't, so didn't—till teeth crunched on my skull.

Robert Penn Warren

The Magical Mouse

I am the magical mouse
I don't eat cheese
I eat sunsets
And the tops of trees
I don't wear fur
I wear funnels
Of lost ships and the weather
That's under dead leaves
I am the magical mouse
I don't fear cats
Or woodsowls
I do as I please
Always
I don't eat crusts
I am the magical mouse
I eat
Little birds—and maidens

That taste like dust

Kenneth Patchen

Where Two O'Clock Came From

The seventh dragon turned to his wife,
And, brushing a cloud out of her hair,
Said, If you think that much coal
Will last the winter, then you ought
To have your scales rechecked.
She burst into fire
And her tongue singed the beard
Of a crabby old gelbus who had his home
In a hollow hole. He sighed wearily
And quick-tailed the sky down.
You should not have done that,
The dragon's wife said; it looks pretty
Bare the way it is up there now.
But they could see some creatures
Sitting at a big table in the air,
And they were fumbling around
With something that looked like a clock.
It's a clock! shouted the old gelbus—
(No flies on him)—What time is it, boys?
We haven't decided yet, they yelled happily.
Make it nice and early, said the dragon;
And his wife called up, That suits me, too.
Then two it is, the creatures sang merrily,
Putting their faces inside the clock
And upsetting the table in their eagerness to find it.

Kenneth Patchen

Overheard on a Saltmarsh

Nymph, nymph, what are your beads?
Green glass, goblin. Why do you stare at them?
Give them me.
         No.
Give them me. Give them me.
            No.
Then I will howl all night in the reeds,
Lie in the mud and howl for them.

Goblin, why do you love them so?

They are better than stars or water,
Better than voices of winds that sing,
Better than any man's fair daughter,
Your green glass beads on a silver ring.

Hush I stole them out of the moon.

Give me your beads, I desire them.
           No.
I will howl in a deep lagoon
For your green glass beads, I love them so.
Give them me. Give them.
        No.

Harold Monro

The Mewlips

The shadows where the Mewlips dwell
　　Are dark and wet as ink,
And slow and softly rings their bell,
　　As in the slime you sink.

You sink into the slime, who dare
　　To knock upon their door,
While down the grinning gargoyles stare
　　And noisome waters pour.

Beside the rotting river-strand
　　The drooping willows weep,
And gloomily the gorcrows stand
　　Croaking in their sleep.

Over the Merlock Mountains a long and weary way,
　In a mouldy valley where the trees are grey,
By a dark pool's borders without wind or tide,
　Moonless and sunless, the Mewlips hide.

The cellars where the Mewlips sit
　　Are deep and dank and cold
With single sickly candle lit;
　　And there they count their gold.

Their walls are wet, their ceilings drip;
   Their feet upon the floor
Go softly with a squish-flap-flip,
   As they sidle to the door.

They peep out slyly; through a crack
   Their feeling fingers creep,
And when they've finished, in a sack
   Your bones they take to keep.

Beyond the Merlock Mountains, a long and lonely road,
   Through the spider-shadows and the marsh of Tode,
And through the wood of hanging trees and the gallows-weed,
   You go to find the Mewlips—and the Mewlips feed.

                                    J. R. R. Tolkien

WORDS
OVERHEARD

Bee! I'm expecting you!

Bee! I'm expecting you!
Was saying Yesterday
To Somebody you know
That you were due—

The Frogs got Home last Week—
Are settled, and at work—
Birds, mostly back—
The Clover warm and thick—

You'll get my Letter by
The seventeenth; Reply
Or better, be with me—
Yours, Fly.

Emily Dickinson

The Last Word of a Bluebird

As told to a child

As I went out a Crow
In a low voice said, "Oh,
I was looking for you.
How do you do?
I just came to tell you
To tell Lesley (will you?)
That her little Bluebird
Wanted me to bring word
That the north wind last night
That made the stars bright
And made ice on the trough
Almost made him cough
His tail feathers off.
He just had to fly!
But he sent her Good-by,
And said to be good,
And wear her red hood,
And look for skunk tracks
In the snow with an ax—
And do everything!
And perhaps in the spring
He would come back and sing."

Robert Frost

Father and I in the Woods

"Son,"
My father used to say,
"Don't run."

"Walk,"
My father used to say,
"Don't talk."

"Words,"
My father used to say,
"Scare birds."

So be:
It's sky and brook and bird
And tree.

David McCord

Conversation

"Mother, may I stay up tonight?"
"No, dear."
"Oh dear! (She always says 'No, dear').
But Father said I might."
"No, dear."
"He did, that is, if you thought it right."
"No, dear, it isn't right."
"Oh dear! Can I keep on the light?"
"No, dear. In spite
Of what your Father said,
You go to bed,
And in the morning you'll be bright
And glad instead
For one more day ahead."
"I might,
But not for one more night."
"No, dear—*no, dear.*"
"At least I've been polite, I guess."
"Yes, dear, you've been polite—
Good night."
"Oh dear,
I'd rather stay down here—
I'm quite . . ."
"No, dear. Now, out of sight."
("Well that was pretty near—")
"*Good* night."
("—all right.")
"Good *night!*"

David McCord

The Parrot

The parrot is a thief.
No word
Is safe in earshot
Of that bird.

He picks it up.
He turns it round.
He croaks.
He tries it out for sound

And then he says it,
Loud and clear,
And all the neighbors
Know you swear.

Edward Lucie-Smith

The Gossip

I'm a green bird.
—David Wagoner

This is no green bird, but gray with bright red
Tail and white chest. Polylingual, our gray

Can mimic the sound of every object:
At night, after the lights are put out, we hear

Silverware clinking on plates, the faucets
Going on and off. It's almost too much

When I hear myself on the telephone,
Or the doorbell ring. He has our life down

In his throat. Listening there in the dark
We fear what he could pick up next—the sounds

He might hear when he has gone through the noise
Of the evening. We know he's sitting there,

Waiting for something special to repeat
When he reaches for us in our sleep.

Daniel Halpern

The Flattered Flying Fish

Said the Shark to the Flying Fish over the phone:
"Will you join me tonight? I am dining alone.
Let me order a nice little dinner for two!
And come as you are, in your shimmering blue."

Said the Flying Fish: "Fancy remembering me,
And the dress that I wore at the Porpoises' tea!"
"How could I forget?" said the Shark in his guile:
"I expect you at eight!" and rang off with a smile.

She has powdered her nose; she has put on her things;
She is off with one flap of her luminous wings.
O little one, lovely, light-hearted and vain,
The Moon will not shine on your beauty again!

E. V. Rieu

Roosters

"Get out of my way!"
    says Rooster One.
"I won't!"
    says Rooster Two.
"You won't?"
"I won't!"
"You shall!"
"I shan't!"
Cock cock a
doodle doo!

They pecked.
They kicked.
They fought for hours.
There was a great
to-do!
"You're a very fine fighter,"
    says Rooster One.
"You're right!"
    says Rooster Two.

Elizabeth Coatsworth

Little Fan

"I don't like the look of little Fan, mother,
    I don't like her looks a little bit.
Her face—well, it's not exactly different,
    But there's something wrong with it.

"She went down to the sea-shore yesterday,
    And she talked to somebody there,
Now she won't do anything but sit
    And comb out her yellowy hair.

"Her eyes are shiny and she sings, mother,
    Like nobody ever sang before.
Perhaps they gave her something queer to eat,
    Down by the rocks on the shore.

"Speak to me, speak, little Fan dear,
    Aren't you feeling very well?
Where have you been and what are you singing,
    And what's that seaweedy smell?

"Where did you get that shiny comb, love,
    And those pretty coral beads so red?
Yesterday you had two legs, I'm certain,
    But now there's something else instead.

"I don't like the looks of little Fan, mother,
    You'd best go and close the door.
Watch now, or she'll be gone for ever
    To the rocks by the brown sandy shore."

James Reeves

Rat Riddles

There was a gray rat looked at me
with green eyes out of a rathole.

"Hello, rat," I said,
"Is there any chance for me
to get on to the language of the rats?"

And the green eyes blinked at me,
blinked from a gray rat's rathole.

"Come again," I said,
"Slip me a couple of riddles;
there must be riddles among the rats."

And the green eyes blinked at me
and a whisper came from the gray rathole:
"Who do you think you are and why is a rat?
Where did you sleep last night and why do you sneeze on
   Tuesdays? And why is the grave of a rat no deeper than
   the grave of a man?"

And the tail of a green-eyed rat
Whipped and was gone at a gray rathole.

Carl Sandburg

The Telephone

"When I was just as far as I could walk
From here today,
There was an hour
All still
When leaning with my head against a flower
I heard you talk.
Don't say I didn't, for I heard you say—
You spoke from that flower on the window sill—
Do you remember what it was you said?"

"First tell me what it was you thought you heard."

"Having found the flower and driven a bee away,
I leaned my head,
And holding by the stalk,
I listened and I thought I caught the word—
What was it? Did you call me by my name?
Or did you say—
Someone said 'Come'—I heard it as I bowed."

"I may have thought as much, but not aloud."

"Well, so I came."

Robert Frost

Needles and Pins

Black was the color of the peddler's wagon,
And black the doors inside the door
He opened, talking: little doors
On silver hinges, double doors
No bigger than his hand, that waited,
Waited till my mother said,
"And what is that in there?" "Oh,"
Said he, "needles." "But I've got
Needles." "Not like these. Or pins—
Look—with ruby heads. And as
For thimbles—try those on, they fit
Like second fingers." "What's in this one?"
"Scissors, madam—English." "What's
In here?" "The perfect thread." "Aha!"
"Don't laugh. Unbreakable." "I don't
Believe it. Dress goods?" "Why, of course.
With patterns out of Paris." "Pooh!"
"Fancy combs, or plain. Mirrors,
Madam—boxes for your jewelry—"
"Have none." "Don't believe it—here!"
A glass necklace. "No"—shaking
Her head as the tired horse shook his;
And the little doors clicked, and the big one closed,
And off went Rumpelstiltskin, mumbling.

Mark Van Doren

Mother to Son

Well, son, I'll tell you:
Life for me ain't been no crystal stair.
It's had tacks in it,
And splinters,
And boards torn up,
And places with no carpet on the floor—
Bare.
But all the time
I'se been a-climbin' on,
And reachin' landin's,
And turnin' corners,
And sometimes goin' in the dark
Where there ain't been no light.
So, boy, don't you turn back.
Don't you set down on the steps
'Cause you finds it kinder hard.
Don't you fall now—
For I'se still goin', honey,
I'se still climbin',
And life for me ain't been no crystal stair.

Langston Hughes

Wait Till Then

"A dull day."
"And yet it is a day."
"What else? What could it be?"
"Why, nothing."
"Oh."
"You still don't understand, my child.
A dark day is so much more than no day—
Some day, none—"
"I see."
"But you don't see. With eyes as warm as yours,
As moist, as large—"
"And so I should see everything."
"Except nothing. Wait till then."
"When?"
"Forget, forget it. I must hold my tongue."
"No, tell me."
"Will not, cannot. Wait, I say,
Till any light at all is so much more
Than no light—oh, it blinds me, thinking of it,
As this day does, compared. I thank this day
For being. That's enough, that's fire and flame,
That's rockets bursting, that's one great
White ball of brightness breaking, that's
Lightning in the night—it shows the shapes
Of dear things still there—still there—"
"I see them."
"Not as I do, not as I do. Wait."
"Till when?"

Mark Van Doren

ONCE
THERE WAS
AND WAS NOT

The Hare and the Tortoise

"You can't race me," said Johnny the Hare,
"Before you've started I'll be there.
   From the barley field
   To the Farmer's barn
I'll lick you, Sammy, fair and square."

Sammy the Tortoise said, "Wait and see!"
Away he crawled to his family (three),
   Clarence, Creeper,
   And Marmaduke—
They were alike as like could be.

"I've entered, mi-lads, for a steeplechase.
I can't leap over the land apace,
   But if four of us run
   Disguised as one,
I guess I can win this jolly old race.

"Clarence, you hide by the green duck pond;
Creeper, in pigsty a mile beyond.

"The starting line, yon barley stook,
Is just the place for you, Marmaduke.

"And me? I'll hide where I'm needed most
A nose and a half from the winning-post."

Marm and Johnny lined up at the start.
"This race," said Johnny, "is really a farce.
   The wheat I sow
   From my bag as I go
Will be ready to cut by the time you pass."

Bang!—they're off! The Hare at a bound
Rocketed over the billowy ground.
   But when he skirted
   The green duck pond,
The Tortoise was only a yard behind.

And when he came to the old pigsty
They were almost neck and neck—O my!

Poor Johnny the Hare, his field half sown,
Threw off his bag and continued alone,
   Drooping and dropping
   And stooping and stopping
And puffing and panting, terribly blown.

Ten yards from the tape he grew a bit bolder
And casting a careless eye over shoulder,
   "Sam, are you there?"
   Said Johnny the Hare.
"I've won!" said the Tortoise, in front, "I told yer."

Farmer and friends were holding the tape,
And *there* was Sammy, all bowing and scrape
   His head held high—
   What a sock in the eye
For Johnny, who stands with his mouth agape.

"Well done!" said the Farmer. "And now, methinks,
'Tis proper to offer you eats and drinks.
   Will you join me, both?"
   "No!" with an oath
Said Johnny the Hare, and home he slinks.

But later back to the farm he hobbled;
His limbs were still limp, and his brain was fuddled.
As he peered through the window he babbled and bubbled:
   "*Four* Sammies I see
   A-sipping their tea!
   Strikes me
I galloped so fast I'm seeing twice double."

Ian Serraillier

Death of the Cat

Alas! Mowler, the children's pride,
Has slipped on a water-butt, tumbled inside
And died.

The seamstress on her sewing machine
Stitched a shroud of satin sheen.

The carpenter hammered and planed a coffin
Of seasoned oak without a knot in.

The sexton—he loved dear Mowler well—
Mournfully, mournfully tolled the bell.

Few were the prayers the parson spoke.
All he could do, poor fellow, was choke.

But saddest of all in the funeral train
Were the children. Deep were their sorrow and pain,

For they knew, as they followed the churchyard through,
They'd never set eyes on Mowler again.

In silence behind the coffin they stepped,
Solemnly, slowly. Everyone wept

Except
The little mice hid in the hedge—not they!
'Twas not *their* hearts that bled.
"Let's out and play,"
They cried. "Oh, spread
The butter thick on the bread!
Dance in cream cheese right up to our knees,
For the cat is dead!
Hooray!
The cat
       is
         dead!"

Ian Serraillier

The Wooing Frog

The frog lay in the step-child's bed.
At break of dawn he upped and said,
"Now, maiden, will you cut off my head?"

She raised the chopper and cried "Yes!"
Then struck: and lo! the gruesome mess
Was still a frog, no more nor less,

No Prince, restored from witch's spell,
But a cold frog out of a well.
Now what had chanced, to spoil the tale?

James Reeves

After Ever Happily

or The Princess and the Woodcutter*

And they both lived happily ever after . . .
The wedding was held in the palace. Laughter
Rang to the roof as a loosened rafter
Crashed down and squashed the chamberlain flat—
And how the wedding guests chuckled at that!
"You, with your horny indelicate hands,
Who drop your haitches and call them 'ands,
Who cannot afford to buy her a dress,
How dare you presume to pinch our princess—
Miserable woodcutter, uncombed, unwashed!"
Were the chamberlain's words (before he was squashed).
"Take her," said the Queen, who had a soft spot
For woodcutters. "He's strong and he's handsome. Why not?"
"What rot!" said the King, but he dare not object;
The Queen wore the trousers—that's as you'd expect.
Said the chamberlain, usually meek and inscrutable,
"A princess and a woodcutter? The match is unsuitable."
Her dog barked its welcome again and again,
As they splashed to the palace through puddles of rain.
And the princess sighed, "Till the end of my life!"
"Darling," said the woodcutter, "will you be my wife?"
He knew all his days he could love no other,
So he nursed her to health with some help from his mother,
And lifted her, horribly hurt, from her tumble.

A woodcutter, watching, saw the horse stumble.
As she rode through the woods, a princess in her prime
On a dapple-grey horse . . . Now, to finish my rhyme,
I'll start it properly: Once upon a time—

Ian Serraillier

* This is a love story from the Middle Ages. The poet
obviously knew his subject backwards.

The Stone Troll

Troll sat alone on his seat of stone,
And munched and mumbled a bare old bone;
    For many a year he had gnawed it near,
        For meat was hard to come by.
            Done by! Gum by!
In a cave in the hills he dwelt alone,
    And meat was hard to come by.

Up came Tom with his big boots on.
Said he to Troll: "Pray, what is yon?
    For it looks like the shin o' my nuncle Tim,
        As should be a-lyin' in graveyard.
            Caveyard! Paveyard!
This many a year has Tim been gone,
    And I thought he were lyin' in graveyard."

"My lad," said Troll, "this bone I stole.
But what be bones that lie in a hole?
    Thy nuncle was dead as a lump o' lead,
        Afore I found his shinbone.
            Tinbone! Thinbone!
    He can spare a share for a poor old troll;
        For he don't need his shinbone."

Said Tom: "I don't see why the likes o' thee
Without axin' leave should go makin' free
    With the shank or the shin o' my father's kin;
        So hand the old bone over!
            Rover! Trover!
    Though dead he be, it belongs to he;
        So hand the old bone over!"

"For a couple o' pins," says Troll, and grins,
"I'll eat thee too, and gnaw thy shins.
    A bit o' fresh meat will go down sweet!
        I'll try my teeth on thee now.
            Hee now! See now!
    I'm tired o' gnawing old bones and skins;
        I've a mind to dine on thee now."

But just as he thought his dinner was caught,
He found his hands had hold of naught.
    Before he could mind, Tom slipped behind

And gave him the boot to larn him.
    Warn him! Darn him!
A bump o' the boot on the seat, Tom thought,
    Would be the way to larn him.

But harder than stone is the flesh and bone
Of a troll that sits in the hills alone.
    As well set your boot to the mountain's root,
        For the seat of a troll don't feel it.
            Peel it! Heal it!
Old Troll laughed, when he heard Tom groan,
    And he knew his toes could feel it.

Tom's leg is game, since home he came,
And his bootless foot is lasting lame;
    But Troll don't care, and he's still there
        With the bone he boned from its owner.
            Doner! Boner!
Troll's old seat is still the same,
    And the bone he boned from its owner!

J. R. R. Tolkien

The Red Herring

after Cros

There was once a high wall, a bare wall. And
against this wall, there was a ladder,
a long ladder. And on the ground,
under the ladder, there was a red
herring. A dry red herring.

And then a man came along. And in his hands
(they were dirty hands) this man had
a heavy hammer, a long nail
(it was also a sharp nail) and
a ball of string. A thick ball of string.

All right. So the man climbed up
the ladder (right up to the top)
and knocked in the sharp nail:
spluk! Just like that.
Right on top of the wall. The bare wall.

Then he dropped the hammer. It dropped
right down to the ground. And onto the nail
he tied a piece of string, a long
piece of string, and onto the string
he tied the red herring. The dry red herring.

And let it drop. And then he climbed
down the ladder (right down
to the bottom), picked up the hammer
and also the ladder (which was pretty heavy)
and went off. A long way off.

And since then, that red herring, the dry
red herring on the end of the string, which is
quite a long piece, has been
very very slowly swinging and
swinging to a stop. A full stop.

I expect you wonder why I made
up this story, such a simple story. Well,
I did it just to annoy people.
Serious people. And perhaps also
to amuse children. Small children.

George MacBeth

I know some lonely Houses off the Road

I know some lonely Houses off the Road
A Robber'd like the look of—
Wooden barred,
And Windows hanging low,
Inviting to—
A Portico,
Where two could creep—
One—hand the Tools—
The other peep—
To make sure All's Asleep—
Old-fashioned eyes—
Not easy to surprise!

How orderly the Kitchen'd look, by night,
With just a Clock—
But they could gag the Tick—
And Mice won't bark—
And so the Walls—don't tell—
None—will—

A pair of Spectacles ajar just stir—
An Almanac's aware—
Was it the Mat—winked,
Or a Nervous Star?
The Moon—slides down the stair,
To see who's there!

There's plunder—where—
Tankard, or Spoon—
Earring—or Stone—
A Watch—Some Ancient Brooch
To match the Grandmama—
Staid sleeping—there—

Day—rattles—too
Stealth's—slow—
The Sun has got as far
As the third Sycamore—
Screams Chanticleer
"Who's there?"
And Echoes—Trains away,
Sneer—"Where"!
While the old Couple, just astir,
Fancy the Sunrise—left the door ajar!

Emily Dickinson

Legend

The blacksmith's boy went out with a rifle
And a black dog running behind.
Cobwebs snatched at his feet,
Rivers hindered him,
Thorn-branches caught at his eyes to make him blind
And the sky turned into an unlucky opal,
But he didn't mind.
I can break branches, I can swim rivers, I can
stare out any spider I meet,
Said he to his dog and his rifle.

The blacksmith's boy went over the paddocks
With his old black hat on his head.
Mountains jumped in his way,
Rocks rolled down on him,
And the old crow cried, *You'll soon be dead;*
And the rain came down like mattocks.
But he only said
I can climb mountains, I can dodge rocks, I can
shoot an old crow any day.
And he went on over the paddocks.

When he came to the end of the day the sun began falling.
Up came the night ready to swallow him,
Like the barrel of a gun,
Like an old black hat,
Like a black dog hungry to follow him.

Then the pigeon, the magpie and the dove began wailing,
And the grass lay down to pillow him.
His rifle broke, his hat blew away and his dog was gone,
And the sun was falling.

But in front of the night the rainbow stood out on the moun-
　　tain
Just as his heart foretold.
He ran like a hare,
He climbed like a fox,
He caught it in his hands, the colours and the cold—
Like a bar of ice, like the columns of a fountain,
Like a ring of gold.
The pigeon, the magpie and the dove flew up to stare,
And the grass stood up again on the mountain.

The blacksmith's boy hung the rainbow on his shoulder,
Instead of his broken gun.
Lizards ran out to see,
Snakes made way for him,
And the rainbow shone as brightly as the sun.
All the world said, *Nobody is braver, nobody is bolder,*
Nobody else has done
Anything to equal it. He went home as easy as could be
With the swinging rainbow on his shoulder.

Judith Wright

Biographies of the Poets

HILAIRE BELLOC (1870–1953) was born in France to a French barrister and an Englishwoman prominent in the early days of women's suffrage. He was educated at Oxford and later naturalized as an English citizen. For adults he wrote many historical studies and volumes of essays and travel sketches. For children he wrote three volumes of verse: *The Bad Child's Book of Beasts, More Beasts for Worse Children,* and *Cautionary Tales,* all of them parodies of the extremely moral Victorian Sunday-school tales for children.

CHARLES CAUSLEY (1917–   ), born and brought up in North Cornwall, England, is a teacher and poet who writes for both adults and children. In the introduction to his anthology of verse for children, *Dawn to Dusk, Modern Ballads and Story Poems,* he says, "Some poems are best read aloud. Others speak to the inward ear, and answer more clearly to silent reading. But however poems may differ on the surface, they have one important quality in common. They remain, as the painter Pablo Picasso has said of all art, weapons of war against brutality and darkness." His most recent book of original verse for children is *Figgie Hobbin.*

JOHN CIARDI (1916–   ) was born in Boston and educated at Bates, Tufts and the University of Michigan. He was for many years a professor of English at Rutgers and poetry editor of *Saturday Review,* for which he is still a contributing editor. He is well known as a poet, lecturer, and translator of Dante as well as for his poems for children, which he began to write as a way of playing games with his nephews and his own children. His books for children include *The Man Who Sang the Sillies, The Reason for the Pelican,* and *Fast and Slow.* Some of his books contain poems with a limited vocabulary for beginning readers.

ELIZABETH COATSWORTH (1893–   ) was born in Buffalo, New York, and educated at Vassar, Columbia, and Radcliffe. After many years of travel in the Orient, North Africa, and Europe, she settled on a farm in Nobleboro, Maine. She has had a long career as a writer for both adults and children and has written novels and sketches as well as poems. One of her many books for children, *The Cat Who Went to Heaven,* was awarded the Newbery Medal in 1931.

E. E. CUMMINGS (1894–1962) was born in Cambridge, Massachusetts, and educated at Harvard. Best known as a poet, he also wrote plays and a novel, and published a series of "six non-lectures" which he gave at Harvard in 1952. For children he wrote a book of stories called *Fairy Tales.*

WALTER DE LA MARE (1873–1956) was an English poet and novelist, born in Kent, who at seventeen went to work as a bookkeeper for Anglo-American (Standard) Oil. Later he became successful enough as an author to retire to the country with his wife and four children and continue writing. He was a master of the shadowy area between the real and the unreal, believing that "Our one hope is to get away from realism, in the accepted sense. An imaginative experience is not only as real as but far realer than an unimaginative one." Among his books for young people are his retellings of folk tales, *Tales Told Again;* a fantasy, *The Three Royal Monkeys* (originally called *The Three Mulla Mulgars*); and *Rhymes and Verses,* which contains most of his poems for children.

EMILY DICKINSON (1830–1886) was born in Amherst, Massachusetts, and educated in local schools and at Mt. Holyoke Female Seminary. She led an active social life in her youth, but withdrew from all but family and close friends in her late twenties. Only 7 of her 1,775 poems were published during her lifetime, and those anonymously, but in this century she has become one of America's best-loved poets.

NORMA FARBER (1909–   ), a concert singer as well as a writer, was born in Boston, educated at Wellesley and Radcliffe, and now lives in Cambridge, Massachusetts. She has written several volumes of poems for adults, including *The Hatch* and *A Desperate*

Thing, and with Edith Holman has translated some of the love poems of the Spanish poet Pedro Salinas, published in a volume called *To Live in Pronouns.* Among her books for children are *Where's Gomer?,* a loose, amusing adaptation of the story of Noah's ark, and *As I Was Crossing Boston Common,* an alphabet of exotic animals, which was nominated for a National Book Award. Two more are scheduled for publication: *A Ship in a Storm on the Way to Tarshish* and *Six Impossible Things Before Breakfast.*

ROBERT FROST (1874–1963), though best known as a New England poet because he settled there and wrote in a New England idiom, was born in San Francisco, where he must have been told as a child that "some of the blowing dust was gold." It was not until after his first book of poems, *A Boy's Will,* was published in England in 1913 that he became famous in America. He never finished college, but often taught or served as poet-in-residence—at Amherst, Dartmouth, the University of Michigan, and Harvard. During his lifetime he was honored with four Pulitzer Prizes, many honorary degrees, and formal felicitations from the U. S. Senate on his seventy-fifth and eighty-fifth birthdays.

NIKKI GIOVANNI (1943–   ), a black feminist poet who writes for adults as well as for children, was born in Knoxville, Tennessee, grew up in Cincinnati, and attended Fisk University. She has taught at Queens College, New York, and at Rutgers. She has written several books of poems, including a volume for children called *ego-tripping,* and an autobiography, *Gemini,* which was a candidate for a National Book Award. She is the mother of a young son, Tommy.

ROBERT GRAVES (1895–   ) is an Englishman of Anglo-Irish family, who has lived for a long time on the island of Majorca. Though he has written novels, essays, criticism, translations, lectures, stories, an autobiography, and a reference book of Greek mythology, he considers himself first of all a poet. In 1961 he was elected to the Chair of Poetry at Oxford. *The Penny Fiddle* contains his poems for children.

DONALD HALL (1928–   ), poet, teacher, editor, and critic, was born in Hamden, Connecticut, and educated at Harvard and Oxford. His book *The Alligator Bride* includes selections from several earlier volumes of poems. He has also written a biography of the sculptor Henry Moore and a book of memoirs, *String Too Short to Be Saved.* His one book for children, *Andrew the Lion Farmer,* was written for his son Andrew, when he was four. Though he is a professor at the University of Michigan, he spends as much time as possible on the New Hampshire farm which once belonged to his grandfather.

DANIEL HALPERN (1945–   ) was born in Syracuse, New York, but grew up in Los Angeles and Seattle. He has also lived in Tangier. He was educated at Columbia and teaches at the New School for Social Research in New York City. He has published poems in such magazines as *The New Yorker* and *Saturday Review,* and in a volume called *Traveling on Credit.*

JUDITH HEMSCHEMEYER (1935–   ) was born in Wisconsin and educated at both the University of Wisconsin and the University of Grenoble, in France. She has worked as a copy-editor for Time, Inc., has lived with her husband and children in Greece, and now teaches at the University of Utah. She has published two volumes of poems, *I Remember the Room Was Filled with Light* and *Very Close and Very Slow,* and a book for children, *Trudie and the Milch Cow.*

HYACINTHE HILL [Virginia Anderson] (1920–   ) was born in New York and educated at Brooklyn and Hunter colleges and Fordham University. Since 1963 she has taught English in New York City. Her poems have appeared in *Etc., A Review of General Semantics,* and she has also published a volume of poems, *Arms and the Woman.*

LANGSTON HUGHES (1902–1967), born in Joplin, Missouri, was educated at Columbia, and Lincoln University in Pennsylvania. His poems, which are strongly ethnic, were written in the spirit of jazz or show kinship to spirituals and blues. The *Langston Hughes Reader,* 1958, contains a cross-section of his work, which includes stories, essays, plays, song lyrics, and autobiography, as well as poetry.

TED HUGHES (1930–   ), a native of Yorkshire, England, was educated at Cambridge University, where he met the American poet Sylvia Plath, whom he later married. His *Selected Poems, 1957– 1967* includes poems from *The Hawk in the Rain, Lupercal,* and *Wodwo. Crow* was published in 1971. Many of his poems use birds of prey as symbols. Among his frequent writings for the BBC is a book of plays for young people, *The Tiger's Bones.* For the same audience he has also written *Season Songs, Poetry Is* and *Meet My Folks,* a collection of monstrously amusing poems about his family.

RANDALL JARRELL (1914–1965) was born in Nashville, Tennessee, and educated at Vanderbilt. From 1947 until his death, he taught English at the Women's College of the University of North Carolina. He also served as poetry consultant for the Library of Congress and as acting literary editor of the *Nation.* Besides his seven books of poems he wrote two volumes of critical essays, *Poetry and the Age* and *A Sad Heart at the Supermarket*; a novel, *Pictures from an Institution*; and three fantasies for children: *The Bat-Poet, The Animal Family,* and *The Gingerbread Rabbit.*

RUTH KRAUSS (1901–   ) was born in Baltimore and studied at the Peabody Conservatory there and at Parsons School of Fine and Applied Art in New York. She married Crockett Johnson, who illustrated some of her books for children. She lives now in Westport, Connecticut. Among her books are *The Backward Day; Bears; Charlotte and the White Horse* and *A Hole Is to Dig,* both illustrated by Maurice Sendak; *The Carrot Seed*; and a book of poems, *The Cantilever Rainbow.*

VACHEL LINDSAY (1879–1931), who was born in Springfield, Illinois, became one of the first American poets to reflect the spirit of the Middle West in poetry. He studied at Hiram College in Ohio and at the Chicago Art Institute. His books of poems, many of which are noted for their jazzlike rhythms, include *General William Booth Enters into Heaven, The Congo and Other Poems, The Chinese Nightingale and Other Poems,* and, especially for children, *Johnny Appleseed and Other Poems.*

DOUGHTRY LONG [Doc Long, Jr.] (1942–   ) was born in Atlanta, Georgia, has lived for two years in Africa, and has traveled extensively in the United States and in the Virgin Islands. His books of poetry include *Black Love, Black Hope* and *Song for Nia.*

EDWARD LUCIE-SMITH (1933–   ) was born in Kingston, Jamaica, and educated in England at King's School, Canterbury, and at Oxford. He is well known not only as a poet but also as an art critic and historian. Two of his books of poems are *A Tropical Childhood* and *Confessions and Histories.*

GEORGE MacBETH (1932–   ), a Scottish poet and editor, was born at Shotts, Lanarkshire, and educated at King Edward School, Sheffield, and at Oxford. He has worked as an editor for the BBC and for Penguin Books. Among his writings are *A Form of Words, The Broken Places, A Doomsday Book,* and *Collected Poems 1958–1970.*

DAVID McCORD (1897–   ), although born in New York City, grew up in the West, living as a boy on a ranch in Oregon and graduating from high school in Portland. He received his BA and MA from Harvard, and later was drama and music writer for the Boston *Transcript.* He has published poems in *The Atlantic, Harper's, Saturday Review,* and *The New Yorker* magazines. His several books of poems for children include *Take Sky, Far and Few, All Day Long, Every Time I Climb a Tree,* and *The Star in the Pail.*

LOUIS MacNEICE (1907–1963) was born in Belfast, Ireland, and attended Oxford, where he became one of a group of important young poets emerging in the 1930's which included W. H. Auden, C. Day Lewis, and Stephen Spender. He became a BBC scriptwriter and producer. His books of poetry include *Ten Burnt Offerings, Visitations, Burning Perch,* and *Collected Poems.*

EVE MERRIAM (1916–   ) was born in Philadelphia and attended Cornell, the University of Pennsylvania, the University of Wisconsin, and Columbia. She lives in New York City, where she has held editorial jobs and has taught creative writing at City College. Outspoken about the issues of her times, including feminism, she has written several books of poems for adults, among them *Family Circle,* which won the prize for the Yale Series of Younger Poets, and *The Double Bed.* Her books for children include *Funny Town, It Doesn't Always Have to Rhyme, Mommies At Work, There Is No Rhyme for Silver,* and *Catch a Little Rhyme.*

EDNA ST. VINCENT MILLAY (1892–1950), one of the best-known lyricists of the first half of this century, was born in Rockland, Maine, and educated at Vassar. Between 1920 and 1950 she published a number of volumes of poems, including *The Harp Weaver and Other Poems,* which won the Pulitzer Prize. She also wrote two biographical works and (with George Dillon) translated Baudelaire's *Flowers of Evil.* Her *Collected Poems* was published posthumously.

A. A. MILNE (1882–1956) was born in London and educated at Cambridge University. Though he preferred to think of himself as an author of novels and plays for adults, his lasting contribution to literature lies in his four books for children, all published in the 1920's. Two are books of verse, *When We Were Very Young* and *Now We Are Six,* and two are collections of stories, *Winnie-the-Pooh* and *The House at Pooh Corner.* These were inspired partly by the childhood and stuffed toys of his son, Christopher Robin, but also by memories of his own childhood.

HAROLD MONRO (1879–1932) was of Scottish descent, but was

born and spent much of his childhood in Belgium. After attending Cambridge University he became involved in various projects to encourage poetry writing, including the Poetry Bookshop in London, a haven for beginning and indigent poets. Although he published several volumes of poems himself, he was most influential as a promoter of poetry. His *Collected Poems* was published after his death.

KENNETH PATCHEN (1911–1972) was born in Ohio, attended the University of Wisconsin, and later lived in California. Interested in a variety of art forms, he illustrated some of his own books and often read his poems to the accompaniment of a jazz group. His books of poems include *When We Were Here Together, Because It Is, But Even So,* and *Collected Poems.*

JAMES REEVES (1909–   ), poet, lecturer, and teacher, was born in North London, educated at Stowe and Cambridge, and now lives in Sussex, England. Formerly a teacher, he has for many years now been a full-time author, editor, and anthologist. He says, "Writing for children and writing about literature demand a continuous exercise of the imagination, a scrupulous insistence on truth of feeling and propriety of language." In addition to a number of critical books on poetry, he has published many retellings of stories from the oral tradition, including *The Cold Flame, Fables from Aesop,* and *English Fables and Fairy Tales, Retold*; some nonsense verse, *Prefabulous Animiles* (with Edward Ardizzone); and two collections of poems for children, *The Blackbird in the Lilac* and *Complete Poems for Children.*

E. V. RIEU (1887–   ) was born in London and educated at St. Paul's School and Oxford. He managed the Oxford University Press in India, was academic and literary adviser to Methuen & Co., Ltd., and was editor of Penguin Classics. He translated the *Iliad* and the *Odyssey* and his whimsical verse for children was published in *The Flattered Flying Fish and Other Poems.*

THEODORE ROETHKE (1908–1963) was born in Saginaw,

Michigan, and grew up there, but was living in Seattle at the time of his death. His father owned a greenhouse, and some of his most appealing poems come from his knowledge of greenhouse life. He taught English at several colleges and universities, coached tennis, and wrote several books of poems for adults: *The Lost Son and Other Poems, The Waking, Words for the Wind,* and *The Far Field,* which was published posthumously. He won a Pulitzer Prize and two National Book Awards. He also published a book of poems for children, *I Am! Says the Lamb.*

CARL SANDBURG (1878–1967), the son of Swedish immigrants, was born in Galesburg, Illinois. He traveled throughout the United States, picking up impressions of America, from farms to steel mills, which he later worked into his poetry. His interest in folklore resulted in his collection of ballads and folksongs, *The American Songbag.* In Kipling's phrase, he called himself "the word of the people." Twice he received the Pulitzer Prize: for *Abraham Lincoln: The War Years* and for his *Complete Poems.* For children he wrote *Rootabaga Stories, Rootabaga Pigeons,* and two books of poems, *Early Moon* and *Wind Song.*

SIEGFRIED SASSOON (1886–1967) was born in London and educated at Marlborough and Cambridge. He is best known for the war poems that rose out of his experience in World War I. After the war he became a pacifist and toured the United States speaking against war. His *Collected Poems,* published in 1947, was followed by *Sequences* in 1956. He also published four autobiographical works.

IAN SERRAILLIER (1912–   ) was born in London, educated at Oxford, and now lives in Sussex, England. He has taught in both public and private schools, and though he wrote only in his spare time until 1962, he has published many poems and stories for children, some of them original, some retellings of old tales. Among his retold legends are *The Ballad of Robin Hood, Beowulf the War-*

rior, and several Greek stories, including *The Gorgon's Head.* His books of poems include *Happily Ever After* and *Belinda and the Swans.*

WILLIAM JAY SMITH (1918–   ) was born in Winnfield, Louisiana, but was brought up in St. Louis, where he went to Washington University. After World War II he studied at Columbia and Oxford, where he was a Rhodes Scholar, and at the University of Florence. He has been a consultant in poetry to the Library of Congress and is at present a professor at Hollins College. He began writing for children in the early 1950's after he heard his four-year-old son chanting rhythmically to himself about a jack-in-the-box. "Children's poetry," he says, "with its wide use of stanza forms and the range of its nonsense, has been for me a liberating influence, giving me a chance to explore in miniature certain themes that I have developed and expanded in adult work." His first book for children, *Laughing Time,* was followed by *Boy Blue's Book of Beasts* and several others. He has also compiled, with Louise Bogan, an anthology of poems for young people, *The Golden Journey.*

RAYMOND SOUSTER (1921–   ) was born in Toronto, Canada, and educated at Humberside Collegiate Institute. He has compiled and edited many volumes of poems and has published more than a dozen volumes of his own, including *The Colour of the Times,* which won Canada's Governor-General Award. Many of his poems are about the city of Toronto, where he is associated with the Canadian Imperial Bank of Commerce.

WILLIAM STAFFORD (1914–   ), a native of Hutchinson, Kansas, was educated at the University of Kansas and the State University of Iowa. He has long lived in Oregon, however, where he teaches English at Lewis and Clark College in Portland. He has published three volumes of poems, including *Traveling through the Dark,* which won the National Book Award.

JAMES STEPHENS (1880–1950) was born and grew up in the

slums of Dublin. He was so poor he had almost no formal schooling, but he became a writer who, like others of the Irish literary renaissance, drew his inspiration from Irish folklore. He was also an authority on Gaelic art and folk music. Though he wrote primarily for adults, much of his work is of interest to children and young people: *Irish Fairy Tales, The Crock of Gold* (a prose fantasy), and *Collected Poems*. His *Deirdre,* the story of a legendary Irish heroine, won the Tallman Gold Medal.

ADRIEN STOUTENBURG (1916–   ) is a native of Minnesota who now makes her home in Lagonitas, California. She has worked as a librarian, free-lance writer, reporter, and editor. Her work for adults includes a volume of poems, *Heroes, Advise Us,* which won the Lamont Poetry Award, and *A Short History of the Fur Trade.* Among her many books for children are *Listen, America, A Life of Walt Whitman* and *American Tall Tales,* retellings of the legends of Paul Bunyan and other legendary heroes.

MAY SWENSON (1919–   ) was born in Logan, Utah, but now lives in New York City. She has been an editor, a lecturer, and a writer-in-residence at Purdue, as well as a poet. She has written fiction and drama and several volumes of poems for adults and has received many awards and honors for her work, including a Guggenheim Fellowship. For children she has written *Poems to Solve.*

J. R. R. TOLKIEN (1892–1973) was born in South Africa but grew up in England and was educated at Oxford, where he later became Merton Professor of English Language and Literature. He was an authority on Old English, Middle English, and Chaucer, and was well known for his scholarly work on *Beowulf* and *Sir Gawain and the Green Knight* before he achieved popularity for his trilogy, *The Lord of the Rings,* and its predecessor, *The Hobbit,* which he read aloud to his children chapter by chapter as he wrote it. In both of these works he combined elements of English and Scandinavian folklore with his own fantasy to create the mythical world of Middle Earth.

MARK VAN DOREN (1894–1972), who was born in Hope, Illinois, and educated at the University of Illinois in Urbana, became one of Columbia University's most distinguished teachers and public lecturers as well as a prolific poet, essayist, and writer of fiction. His *Collected Poems* won the Pulitzer Prize in 1940. Another volume of collected poems appeared in 1963, and two more volumes of lyric poems appeared later. Most of his work was written for adults, but the poems in *The Careless Clock* were written for and about children in the family.

ROBERT PENN WARREN (1905–   ) was born in Guthrie, Kentucky, and educated at Vanderbilt, where he was one of the Fugitive Group of southern writers in the 1920's. In 1950 he went to Yale to teach. There he collaborated with Cleanth Brooks on *Understanding Poetry,* a textbook that revolutionized the teaching of poetry in American colleges. He has published several novels as well as several volumes of poems, has had Guggenheim Fellowships, and has won two Pulitzer Prizes, one for his novel *All the King's Men* and the other for *Promises: Poems 1954–56.*

RUTH WHITMAN (1922–   ) was born in New York City and educated at Radcliffe. She now lives in Cambridge, Massachusetts. She has done editorial work for Houghton Mifflin and for the Harvard University Press and has conducted poetry workshops at the Cambridge Center for Adult Education. She is the translator and compiler of *An Anthology of Modern Yiddish Verse* and a co-translator of *Selected Poems of Alain Bosquet* as well as of Isaac B. Singer's *Short Friday.* Her own poems have been published in *Blood and Milk Poems, The Marriage Wig and Other Poems,* and *The Passion of Lizzie Borden: New and Selected Poems.*

WILLIAM CARLOS WILLIAMS (1883–1963) was born in Rutherford, New Jersey, where as a physician he had a busy general practice all his adult life. He was also a prolific writer of both prose and poetry. He said the practice of medicine gave him access to the "secret gardens of the self" and felt that poetry should see things with "great intensity of perception." *In the American Grain* is perhaps the most significant of his prose works, and the personal epic *Paterson* his most significant poem, but he may be best known for some of his early free-verse lyrics which focus on particular things. Book III of *Paterson* won the first National Book Award, and the Pulitzer Prize was awarded posthumously for *Pictures from Breughel.*

HUMBERT WOLFE (1885–1940), an English poet, playwright, and lampoonist, was born in Milan, Italy, and educated at Oxford. He was deputy secretary of the Ministry of Labour, but called himself "a most uncivil Civil servant" by day and a poet by night. He wrote critical essays in addition to poems. Among his books are *London Sonnets* and *Circular Saws.*

JUDITH WRIGHT (1915–   ) was born in Armidale, New South Wales, and has an Arts degree from the University of Sydney. She has been a part-time lecturer in Australian literature at several universities and has won two Commonwealth Literary Scholarships. She has edited anthologies of Australian poetry and has written a number of books for children and young people, as well as biography, criticism, and books on wildlife conservation. In addition, she has published several volumes of her own poems, which are now available in her *Collected Poems.*

Index of Poets

Index of Titles

Index of First Lines———————————————

Acknowledgments

We would like to thank several young friends who have helped in the making of this book by reading or listening to some of these poems while we were considering them: Abigail and Emily Harrison, Dawn and Diane Kuebler, Susanna Palmer, Nat and Thea Finney, and Andrea Hill. Their opinions and encouragement were most helpful.

In addition, acknowledgment is made to the following for permission to reprint copyrighted material (the publisher regrets it if any acknowledgments have been omitted and would appreciate being advised of this):

Hilaire Belloc: "Rebecca, Who Slammed Doors for Fun and Perished Miserably," from Belloc's *Cautionary Verses,* published 1941 by Alfred A. Knopf, Inc., reprinted by permission of the publisher and The Estate of H. Belloc. Charles Causley: "Riley," from his *Figgie Hobbin,* copyright © 1973 by Charles Causley, reprinted by permission of Walker & Co., Inc., New York, N.Y. John Ciardi: "The Cat Heard the Cat-Bird" and "The Man in the Onion Bed," reprinted by permission of Houghton Mifflin Co. from Ciardi's *I Met a Man,* copyright © 1961 by John Ciardi; "The Man in the Woods," reprinted by permission of J. B. Lippincott Co. from Ciardi's *The Man Who Sang the Sillies,* copyright © 1961 by John Ciardi; "The Pinwheel's Song," reprinted by permission of J. B. Lippincott Co. from Ciardi's *The Reason for the Pelican,* copyright © 1959 by John Ciardi. Elizabeth Coatsworth: "A Lady Comes to an Inn," reprinted by permission of Coward, McCann & Geoghegan, Inc., from Coatsworth's *The Creaking Stair,* copyright 1923 by Elizabeth Coatsworth, 1929, 1949 by Coward-McCann, Inc., renewed; "Roosters," reprinted by permission of Macmillan Publishing Co., Inc., from Coatsworth's *Poems,* copyright © 1957 by Macmillan Publishing Co., Inc. E. E. Cummings: "hist whist," copyright 1923, 1951 by E. E. Cummings, and "who knows if the moon's," copyright 1925 by E. E. Cummings, both reprinted by permission of Harcourt Brace Jovanovich, Inc., from *Complete Poems, 1913–1962* by E. E. Cummings. Walter de la Mare: "Jim Jay" and "Mistletoe," reprinted by permission of The Literary Trustees of Walter de la Mare, and The Society of Authors as their representative, from de la Mare's *Collected Rhymes and Verses,* published by Faber & Faber, Ltd., 1944. Emily Dickinson: Poem #288 ("I'm Nobody! Who are you?"), Poem #289 ("I know some lonely Houses off the Road"), and Poem #1035 ("Bee! I'm expecting you"), reprinted by permission of the publishers and the Trustees of Amherst College from *The Poems of Emily Dickinson,* edited by Thomas H. Johnson, published by The Belknap Press of Harvard University Press, Cambridge, Mass., copyright 1951, © 1955 by the President and Fellows of Harvard College. Norma Farber: "The Hatch," reprinted by permission of Charles Scribner's Sons from *The Hatch: Poems, Poets of Today II,* © 1955 by Norma Farber. Robert Frost: "A Peck of Gold," "The Last Word of a Bluebird," and "The Telephone," reprinted by permission of Holt, Rinehart and Winston from *The Poetry of Robert Frost,* edited by Edward Connery Lathem, copyright 1916, 1928, © 1969 by Holt, Rinehart and Winston, copyright 1944, © 1956 by Robert Frost. Nikki Giovanni: "Knoxville, Tennessee," reprinted by permission of William Morrow & Co., Inc., from her *Black Feeling, Black Talk, Black Judgement,* copyright © 1968, 1970 by Nikki Giovanni. Robert Graves: "Henry and Mary" (copyright 1923, 1929, 1939, © 1955, 1958, 1961, 1966 by Robert Graves) and "The Bedpost" (copyright 1923, 1929, 1939, © 1955, 1958, 1961 by Robert Graves), both published in

Whipperginny, Alfred A. Knopf, 1923; also "The Two Witches" (copyright ©
1966 by Robert Graves), published in *Collected Poems, 1966,* Doubleday & Co.,
Inc.; also "Warning to Children" (copyright 1939, © 1955, 1958, 1961, 1966 by
Robert Graves), published in *Collected Poems,* Random House, 1939—all reprinted by permission of Curtis Brown, Ltd. Donald Hall: "Self-portrait, As a
Bear," copyright © 1962 by Donald Hall, reprinted by permission of the author
from his *The Alligator Bride,* Harper & Row, 1969. Daniel Halpern: "The Gos-
sip," reprinted by permission of The Viking Press from his *Traveling on Credit,*
copyright © 1972 by Daniel Halpern. Hyacinthe Hill: "Rebels from Fairy Tales,"
reprinted by permission of the author from *Etc.: A Review of General Semantics,*
copyright © 1967 by Hyacinthe Hill. Judith Hemschemeyer: "The Settlers," reprinted by permission of Wesleyan University Press from *I Remember the Room
Was Filled with Light,* copyright © 1973 by Judith Hemschemeyer. Langston
Hughes, "Mother to Son," copyright 1926 and renewed 1954 by Langston Hughes,
reprinted from his *Selected Poems* by permission of Alfred A. Knopf, Inc. Randall
Jarrell: "A Sick Child," reprinted by permission of Farrar, Straus & Giroux, Inc.,
from his *The Complete Poems,* copyright 1949 by Mrs. Randall Jarrell, copyright
renewed © 1977 by Mary von Schrader Jarrell. Ruth Krauss: "Song," copy-
right © 1965, 1976 by Ruth Krauss, reprinted by permission of the author from her
The Cantilever Rainbow, Pantheon Books, 1965. Vachel Lindsay: "The Haughty
Snail-King," reprinted by permission of Macmillan Publishing Co., Inc., from
his *Collected Poems,* copyright 1914 by Macmillan Publishing Co., Inc., renewed
1942 by Elizabeth C. Lindsay. Doughtry Long: "#4," reprinted by permission of
Broadside Press from *Black Love, Black Hope,* copyright © 1971 by Doughtry
Long. Edward Lucie-Smith: "The Parrot," reprinted by permission of the author,
copyright © 1972 by Edward Lucie-Smith. David McCord: "Conversation," copyright 1941 by David McCord, and "Father and I in the Woods," copyright 1952
by David McCord—both reprinted by permission of Little, Brown & Co. from
McCord's *Far and Few.* Louis MacNeice: "Invocation," reprinted by permission
of Faber & Faber, Ltd., and Oxford University Press, Inc., from *The Collected
Poems of Louis MacNeice,* edited by E. R. Dodds, copyright © 1966 by The
Estate of Louis MacNeice. Eve Merriam: "Alligator on the Escalator," reprinted
by permission of Atheneum Publishers from her *Catch a Little Rhyme,* copyright
© 1966 by Eve Merriam. Edna St. Vincent Millay: "A Visit to the Asylum,"
reprinted by permission of Norma Millay Ellis from *Collected Poems* (Harper &
Row, 1956), copyright 1923, 1951 by Edna St. Vincent Millay and Norma Millay
Ellis. A. A. Milne: "Halfway Down," reprinted by permission of E. P. Dutton
& Co., Inc., from his *When We Were Very Young,* illustrated by Ernest H.
Shepard; copyright 1924 by E. P. Dutton & Co., renewal 1952 by A. A. Milne.
Harold Monro: "Overheard on a Saltmarsh," reprinted by permission of Gerald
Duckworth & Co., Ltd., from his *Collected Poems,* copyright © 1970 by Gerald
Duckworth & Co., Ltd. Kenneth Patchen: "A Trueblue Gentleman," "The Magi-
cal Mouse," and "Where Two O'Clock Came From," reprinted by permission of
New Directions Publishing Corp. from Patchen's *Collected Poems,* copyright
1943, 1952 by Kenneth Patchen. James Reeves: "Little Fan" and "Mr. Tom
Narrow," reprinted by permission of William Heinemann, Ltd., Publishers, from
Reeves' *The Wandering Moon;* "The Horn," reprinted by permission of the
author from his *The Blackbird in the Lilac,* published in 1952 by Oxford University Press, copyright 1952 by James Reeves; "The Wooing Frog," reprinted
by permission of William Heinemann, Ltd., Publishers, from Reeves' *The Talking Skull.* E. V. Rieu: "The Flattered Flying Fish," "The Green Train," "The
Paint Box," and "Tony the Turtle," reprinted by permission of Richard Rieu,
Literary Executor, from *The Flattered Flying Fish and Other Poems* by E. V.